Contents

Page

Moving and Growing

Skeletons

Humans can stand up because they have a skeleton. The skeleton does three things:

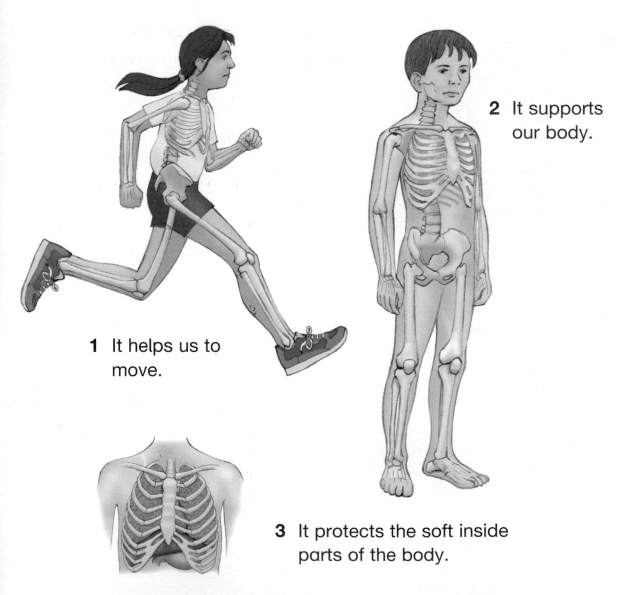

2 It supports our body.

1 It helps us to move.

3 It protects the soft inside parts of the body.

There are two types of skeletons: **endoskeletons** and **exoskeletons**.

Humans have endoskeletons which means that the bones are inside the body.

This is a human skeleton. The names of some common bones are shown.

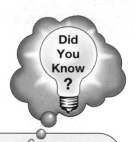

Did You Know ?

- Your skeleton is made up of about 200 bones.
- Muscles make up between 40% and 50% of a person's body weight.
- The skeleton is able to move in different ways because of the different types of joints it contains.

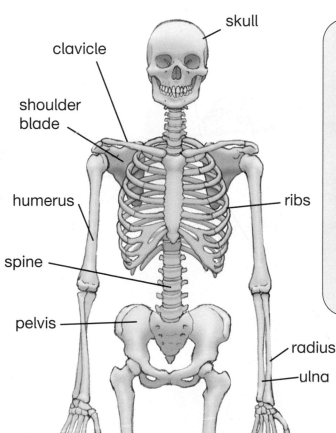

skull
clavicle
shoulder blade
humerus
spine
pelvis
ribs
radius
ulna
femur
patella (knee cap)
shin bone
fibula

Remember

- Fish, amphibia, birds and mammals have skeletons inside their bodies. They have an endoskeleton.

Skeletons of Other Animals

The human skeleton is designed for walking and running. It can hold things in its hand.

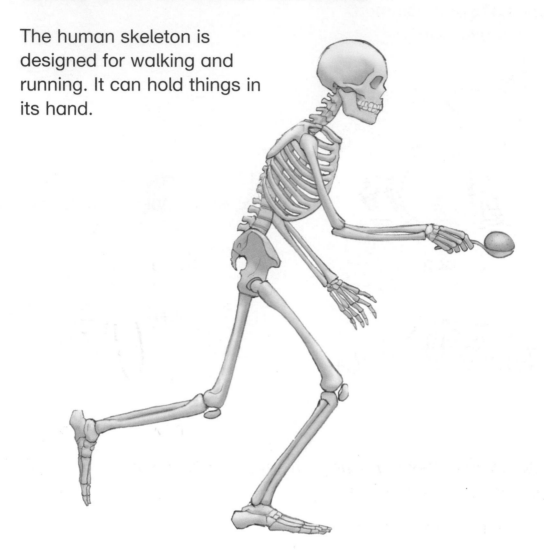

The skeletons of other animals are designed for different ways of life.

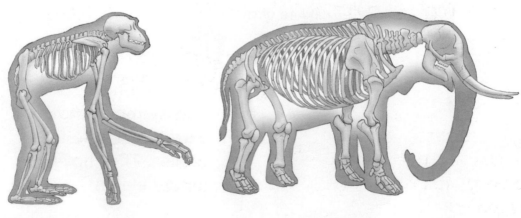

chimpanzee   elephant

Here are the skeletons of other vertebrates (animals with backbones).

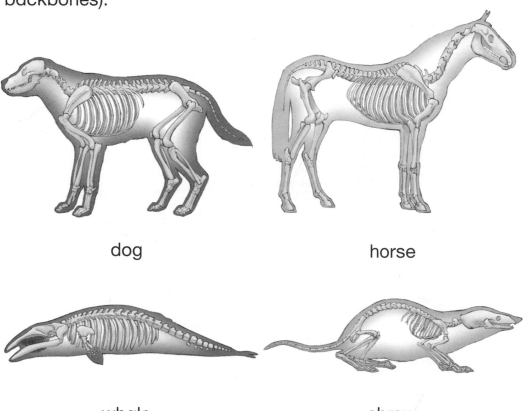

dog horse

whale shrew

Write down at least two ways in which each animal is adapted to the way it lives.

Use these words to help you.

| tall | long | running | swinging |
| swimming | holding | reaching | gripping |

Did You Know?

- The smallest bones in the body are inside your ear.

Remember

- Humans and other vertebrates have skeletons to help them move.

Muscles

Muscles are attached to bones in the body by strong cords called **tendons**.

Muscles work by contracting (getting shorter) and relaxing (getting longer).

This diagram shows what happens to the muscles in your arm when you lift something.

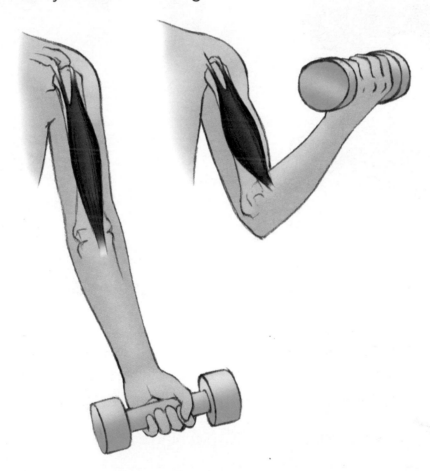

Things to do

1 Hold a ball in your arm and then lift from the elbow.

2 Feel the top arm muscle to see what happens to it when you lift the ball.

3 Draw a picture to show what your arm muscle looks like when you flex your elbow.

The skeleton can move because it contains **joints.**

The joints are found where two bones meet. They allow the body to move in different directions.

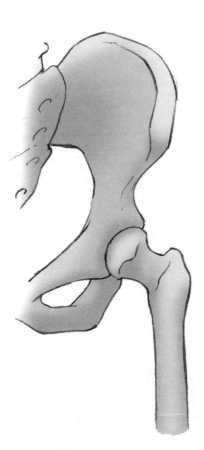

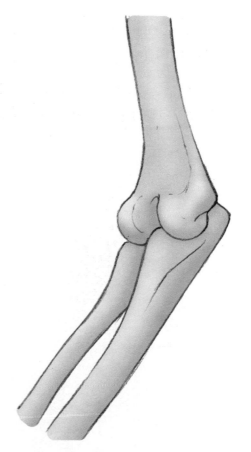

This is a hip joint. It is a ball and **socket joint** and works like the joint on the driver's mirror in a car.

This is an elbow joint. It is a **hinge joint** and works like the hinge on a door.

Did You Know ?

- About 40–50% of the weight of an animal is made up of muscles.

Remember

- Animals have muscles to help support and move their bodies.

Alison and Vikram's Experiment

Alison and Vikram carried out an experiment to see how far their friends could jump.

Each person started from the same point and used a standing jump.

This table shows the results of the experiment.

Name	Length of leg from hip to ankle (cm)	First jump (cm)	Second jump (cm)	Third jump (cm)	Average (cm)
Nick	54	62	63	65	63
John	58	85	80	88	84
Lauren	53	56	65	66	62
Sunita	60	72	70	68	70
Vikram	55	54	58	57	56
Alison	45	62	65	66	64

Questions

1 Which child had the longest legs?

2 Which child jumped the furthest?

3 Why do you think the children jumped three times?

4 Did the person with the longest legs jump the furthest?

5 Draw a bar chart to show the results of the experiment.

Remember

- The legs contain strong muscles to help them move.

Habitats

Habitats for Invertebrates

Different **invertebrates** (animals without backbones) live in different **habitats**.

Follow the questions on this key to help you find out the names of invertebrates.

Invertebrate Key

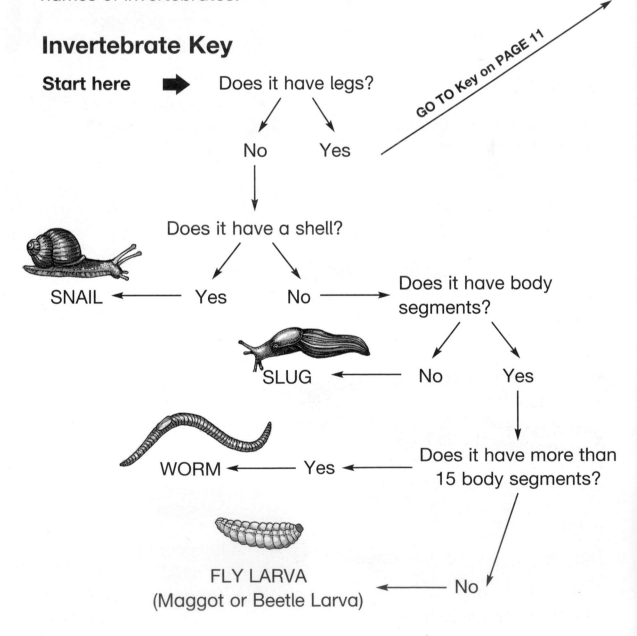

Start here ➡ Does it have legs?

GO TO Key on PAGE 11

No   Yes

Does it have a shell?

SNAIL ⟵ Yes   No ⟶ Does it have body segments?

SLUG ⟵ No   Yes

WORM ⟵ Yes ⟵ Does it have more than 15 body segments?

FLY LARVA
(Maggot or Beetle Larva) ⟵ No

Invertebrate key (with legs)

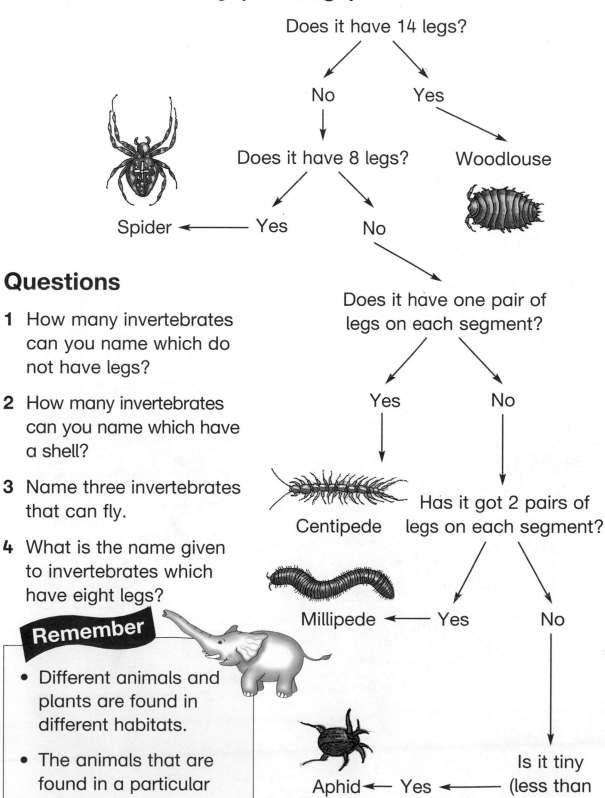

Does it have 14 legs?

No   Yes

Does it have 8 legs?   Woodlouse

Spider ← Yes   No

Does it have one pair of
legs on each segment?

Yes   No

Centipede   Has it got 2 pairs of
legs on each segment?

Millipede ← Yes   No

Aphid ← Yes ← Is it tiny
(less than
2 mm)?

Questions

1 How many invertebrates
can you name which do
not have legs?

2 How many invertebrates
can you name which have
a shell?

3 Name three invertebrates
that can fly.

4 What is the name given
to invertebrates which
have eight legs?

Remember

- Different animals and
plants are found in
different habitats.

- The animals that are
found in a particular
habitat are suited to
living there.

Pond Dipping

Chris, Alison and Lee are investigating a local habitat.

They want to find out what lives in and around the local pond.

What do you think they might find?

A

These are some of the things that they found.

B

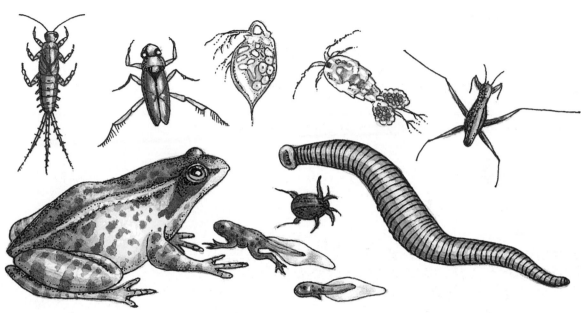

Questions

1 If the children dipped the pond in winter do you think they would find the same organisms? Give a reason for your answer.

2 What do you think frogs eat? Make a list.

3 Try to draw a food chain showing the creatures above. Remember food chains always start with a green plant.

4 How do you think the creatures got into the pond in the first place? Try discussing this question with a friend before telling your teacher the answer.

Remember

- The animals and plants that live around a pond are suited to living there.

- In a pond there are more smaller organisms than larger ones. Often the larger organisms feed on the smaller ones.

Data Gathering

When Chris, Alison and Lee had finished dipping the pond they counted how many organisms they had found.

Here is the tally chart they made.

Name	1	2	3	4	5	6	7	8	9	10	11	12	13	14	15	16	17	18	19
Frog	✓	✓	✓																
Tadpole	✓	✓	✓	✓	✓	✓													
Pond skater	✓	✓																	
Mayfly nymph	✓	✓	✓	✓															
Water mite	✓	✓	✓	✓	✓	✓	✓	✓	✓										
Cyclops	✓	✓	✓	✓	✓	✓	✓	✓	✓	✓	✓								
Daphnia	✓	✓	✓	✓	✓	✓	✓	✓	✓	✓	✓	✓	✓	✓	✓	✓			
Leech	✓	✓	✓																
Great diving beetle	✓	✓	✓	✓	✓	✓													
Dragon fly	✓	✓																	
Caddis fly larvae	✓	✓	✓	✓	✓	✓													

Things to do

1 Draw a bar chart to show the results of the pond dip.

2 Ask your teacher if you can survey your local pond or another habitat to see what you can find.

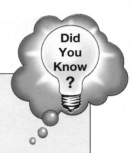

Did You Know ?

- You can find water life in all kinds of habitats.

- Even an old washing up bowl left outside for a couple of months will begin to have a variety of life in it!

- You can visit all kinds of places to see water life.

- Reservoirs and dams often have displays of the water life that lives locally.

- Fish farms are interesting places to visit, particularly when the fish are being fed.

- Aquariums contain a good variety of water life. Not just the big fish, but also the small water creatures that you have seen in a school pond.

Questions

1 Which organism had the highest total?

2 Why do you think the children saw only two dragonflies?

3 Why were there more tadpoles than frogs?

4 Draw a food chain to show what the children found in the pond.

Remember

- It is possible to estimate the numbers of organisms that live in a habitat by taking a sample.

- Food chains show what feeds on what in a habitat.

Other Habitats

Here are different types of habitat. Can you name them all?

A

B

C

D

E

F

Which one of these habitats is not found in this country?

Sometimes habitats are destroyed.

This can be because the land is wanted for another use, or has been polluted.

Imagine what would happen to this woodland habitat and all the animals that live there if it was cleared to make way for a new road.

Things to do

1 Where do you think all the animals and plants would go?

2 Write a letter to the local council telling them how you feel about the new road.

Remember

- Habitats can be destroyed and this affects the organisms that live there.

Keeping Warm

Measuring Temperature

Temperature is measured using a **thermometer**.
The units of temperature are degrees Celsius (°C).

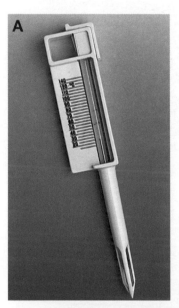

A

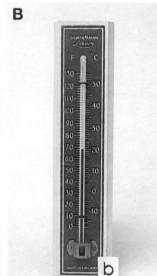

B

C

D

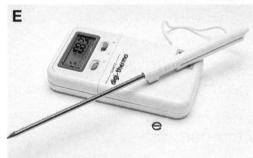

E

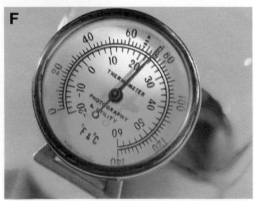

F

Situation	Typical Temp. (°C)
ice/water	0
cold tap water	8
room temperature	20
normal body temperature	37
hot tap water	45
boiling water	100
burning match	400

Questions

1 Look back at the photographs of the thermometers. Which thermometer would be the best to measure each of the following? For each one choose a letter (A–F).
   a) the temperature of the ground, measured every 5 minutes for 24 hours.
   b) a baby's temperature
   c) the temperature in a house
   d) the temperature of a burning match

2 What sort of temperature would you expect the following to have?
   a) a cold winter's day with snow on the ground
   b) a hot bath or shower of water
   c) a hot cup of tea
   d) a burning firework.

Remember

- Temperature is measured using thermometers.

- Temperature is measured in degrees Celsius (°C).

Temperature and the Weather

The temperature around us changes during the day and from day to day.

It is usually hotter during the daytime than it is at night.

It is also usually hotter in summer than in winter.

A

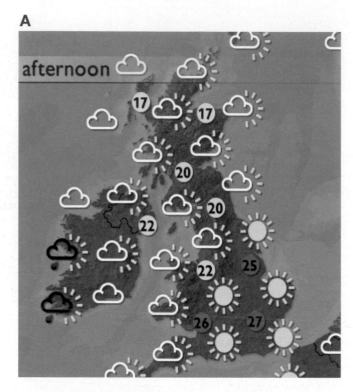

The United Kingdom in summer.

B

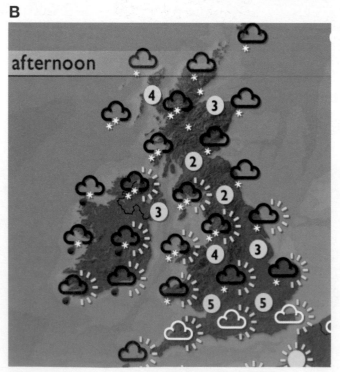

The United Kingdom in winter.

Pictures A and B are weather maps. Each map shows the temperatures in different parts of the UK.

A typical room temperature in the summer is 20°C.

If a glass containing ice is left in a room it will melt and become water. The water will warm up until it is the same temperature as the room.

If a glass containing boiling water is left in a room it will cool down. Eventually the water will have the same temperature as the room.

0 degrees C   90 degrees C

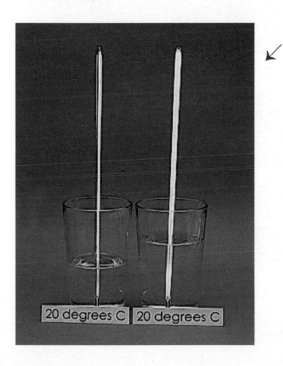

20 degrees C   20 degrees C

Questions

1 Look at weather map A. Estimate the temperature outside your school on the day this weather map was printed.

2 Look at weather map B. Estimate the temperature outside your school on the day this weather map was printed.

Remember

- Temperatures are usually higher in summer than in winter.

- Temperatures are usually higher in the daytime than at night.

- Room temperature is often about 20°C.

- Objects cool or warm to the temperature of their surroundings.

Thermal Insulators

Some materials let heat pass through them very quickly.

The metal in a saucepan is a good example of this type of material.

These materials are called **thermal conductors**.

Other materials do not let heat pass through very quickly.

The wooden handle of a saucepan is a good example of this type of material.

These materials are called **thermal insulators**.

Air itself can be a good insulator providing it cannot move about. Many of the materials shown below can trap air. Some are foams and so the air is trapped when they are made. Other materials trap air in their fibres.

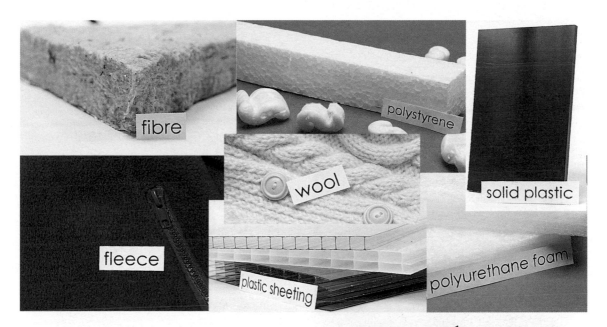

fibre

polystyrene

wool

solid plastic

fleece

plastic sheeting

polyurethane foam

These materials are good insulators.

Questions

1 Name a material which is a good thermal conductor.

2 Name a material which is a good thermal insulator.

3 Where do you think plastic foam is used as an insulator?

4 As well as thermal conductors, there are electrical conductors.
   a) What is an electrical conductor?
   b) Give an example of one.

Remember

- Materials which let heat pass through them quickly are called thermal conductors.

- Materials which do not let heat pass through them quickly are called thermal insulators.

- Many good insulators work because they can trap air.

More Thermal Insulators

Thermal insulators have two main uses:
- they keep warm things warm
- they keep cold things cold.

A

This material reduces the amount of energy lost through the roof of a house.

B

This material reduces the amount of energy lost from the hot water.

C

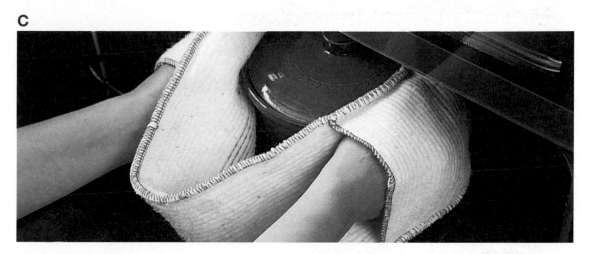

The oven gloves should keep the hands cool!

D

The insulators used here keep cold things cold,
and hot things hot.

Questions

1 What materials are used to
   make oven gloves?

2 What material is used to make
   the jacket that surrounds a hot
   water tank?

3 What material is used to make
   a 'cool box' as shown in
   picture D?

Remember

- Thermal insulators
  keep warm things
  warm and cold things
  cold.

Solids and Liquids

Grouping Solids and Liquids

Scientists find it useful to put materials into groups.
Materials can be grouped according to simple properties.

For example:
Is the material rough? Is the material smooth?
Is the material transparent? Is the material magnetic?
Does the material conduct electricity?

A

Materials can also be grouped into solids and liquids.

Solids	**Liquids**

B

Solids have a fixed shape.

D

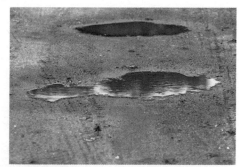

Liquids have no real shape.

C

Solids can sometimes be poured but do not take the shape of the container.

E

Liquids can be poured and always take the shape of the container.

Questions

1 Look at photograph A. Choose a material that is:
a) rough
b) magnetic
c) transparent.

2 Write down the names of three liquids you can see in photograph A.

3 Why is powdered chalk more like a liquid than a lump of chalk is?

Remember

- Materials can be grouped by their properties.

- Solids have a fixed shape.

- Liquids have no shape – they take the shape of the container.

Changing Solids into Liquids

When a solid changes to a liquid we say it **melts**.

When a liquid is cooled to a low temperature it will change back into a solid.

A

Ice will melt when the temperature is above freezing point.

B

Chocolate melts at a low temperature.

C

Candle wax melts because of the heat from the flame.

D

Some metals will melt only at very high temperatures.

Questions

1 When a candle burns, a liquid forms around the wick. What is this liquid?

2 How has this liquid been formed?

3 One of the photographs shows chocolate that has melted in the Sun. Name another substance that melts in the Sun.

4 Look at photograph C. Why are there lumps of candle wax on the sides of the candle?

Remember

- Melting is the change of a solid to a liquid.

- The temperature of a solid has to increase before it will melt.

- Some solids, such as metals, melt at very high temperatures.

- When a liquid is cooled it can turn back into a solid.

Dissolving

When some solids are added to water they seem to disappear. They **dissolve** in the water and form a **solution**.

The solid has not disappeared but it has been broken down by the water into very small pieces that we cannot see.

Some solids do not dissolve in water at all. The water cannot break them down.

Lemonade is a solution. It is made by dissolving sugar and other substances in water.

The paint is not a solution. The paint powder has mixed with the water but it has not dissolved.

Stirring helps things to dissolve. That's why you stir a cup of tea when you put in sugar.

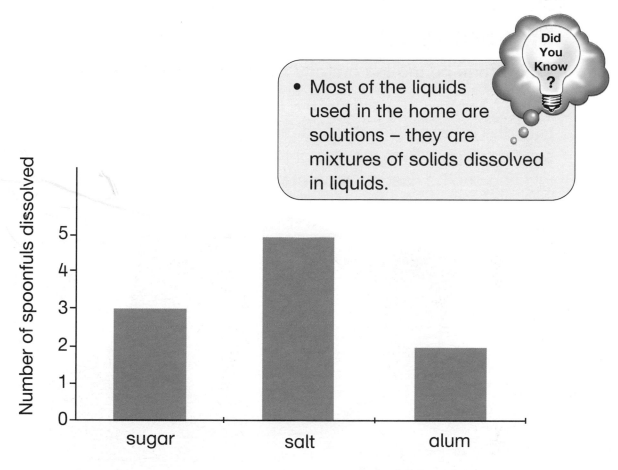

Did You Know?

- Most of the liquids used in the home are solutions – they are mixtures of solids dissolved in liquids.

Questions

1 Name two solids that dissolve in water.

2 Name two solids that **do not** dissolve in water.

3 Name a liquid used in the home that is a solution. Do you know what it contains?

4 Jen and Alice test three solids to see how much will dissolve in a cup of water. Look at their results above. Which solid dissolved the most?

Remember

- A solid dissolves when it is broken down into very small pieces by water.

- Not all solids dissolve.

- Stirring helps solids to dissolve.

- When a solid dissolves in water it forms a solution.

Filters and Filtering

A **filter** can be made from any material that has holes in it.

When a mixture of a solid and a liquid are poured into the filter, the liquid passes through the holes. If the pieces of the solid are bigger than the size of the holes they will be trapped. Filtering can be used to separate a solid from a liquid.

Tea bags have holes that the tea can pass through but not the tea leaves.

How to make a filter

Things to do

1 Find a material that will make a good filter. Explain why you have chosen that material. How could you test it?

2 Filtering is an important part of the process used to purify water. Find out what material is used as a filter in a water filtration plant. (You may be surprised!)

Questions

1 Complete this sentence:
Filtering will separate
a _____ from a
_____ .

2 Do you think a plastic bag will make a good filter? Give a reason for your answer.

3 Which one of the following mixtures could you separate by filtering:
a) salt and water
b) sand and water
c) sugar and water?
Give a reason for your choice.

Remember

- Filtering can be used to separate a solid and a liquid.

- A filter has holes in it.

- Filtering will not remove the solid from a solution – the solid particles in the solution will pass through the holes.

Friction

Friction and Lubricants

Friction is a force which tries to stop things from moving.

In some situations friction can be very useful.

A

There needs to be a high friction force between the tyres and the road.

In other situations friction can be a nuisance.

B

Oil is a **lubricant**. It is used to reduce the friction between the metal parts of the engine.

C

Skiers put wax on their skis to reduce friction.

D

Part of bicycle	How friction helps
handle bar grips	stops the hands from slipping

Questions

1 Why is friction important for racing cars?

2 How do skiers reduce friction?

3 What is a lubricant?

4 Look at picture D. Which parts of the bicycle make use of friction? Complete the table above.

Remember

- Friction is a force which stops things moving.

- Lubricants are used to reduce friction and make things move more easily.

Streamlining

When things move through the air, friction forces slow them down.

These friction forces are called **air resistance**.

When things move through water, friction forces slow them down.

These friction forces are called **water resistance**.

Streamlining is used to reduce friction forces.

A

B

C

D

Streamlining reduces air and water resistance.

E

Most fish have a streamlined shape.

F

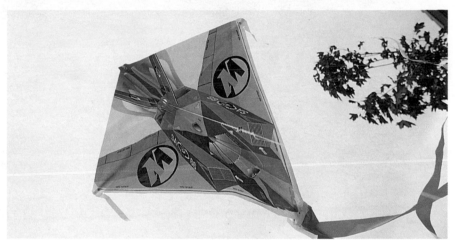

Kites are not streamlined. They are designed to 'catch' the wind.

Questions

1 Why do car manufacturers make streamlined cars?

2 Look at photograph D. Write down two ways the swimmer has reduced her water resistance.

3 What types of shapes are streamlined? Try to describe them.

Remember

- Air resistance and water resistance are both friction forces.

- Streamlining is used to reduce friction forces.

Parachutes

Parachutes make good use of the friction force caused by air resistance.

The wide shape of the parachute makes the friction force as big as possible. This makes the parachute 'catch' the wind.

A

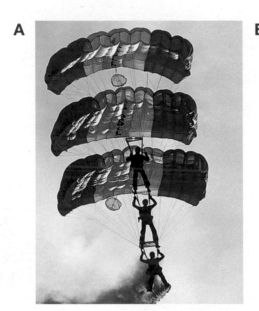

B

The direction of a force can be shown by using arrows.

C

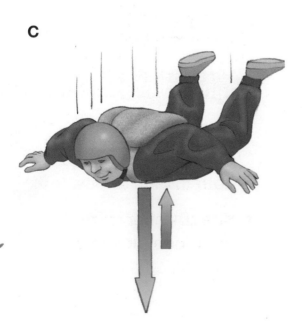

There are two main forces acting on the free-fall parachutist:

1 The force of **gravity** pulls the parachutist to the ground.
2 The force of **air resistance** acts in the opposite direction.

D

a

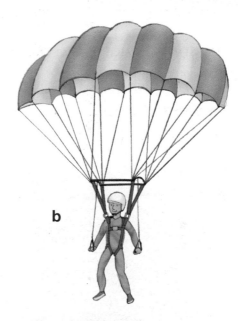

b

Questions

1 What type of a force is air resistance?

2 Look at the two parachutes in picture D. Which do you think will fall slower, a or b? Give a reason for your answer.

3 What do you think would happen if the space shuttle used two parachutes rather than one?

4 Look at the free-falling parachutist in picture C. Why do you think the two arrows are different sizes?

Remember

• Air resistance is a friction force.

• Parachutes are designed to increase air resistance.

• The direction of a force can be shown with an arrow.

Grip

Tyres are designed to grip the road.

Grooves in the tyre allow water to be squeezed away so that the tyre touches the road.

A

This tyre grips the road very well when the road is dry.

B

This tyre gives much better grip when the road is wet.

Shoes are designed to grip the ground.

As with tyres, the grooves allow water to be pushed away.

C

These boots are designed to give good grip in dry and wet weather.

D

These skates are designed to have very little grip!

E

F

Questions

1 Look at the shoes in picture E. Which shoe do you think will give the best grip? Give a reason for your answer.

2 Look at the trainers in picture F. Which trainer do you think will give the best grip in wet weather? Give a reason for your answer.

Remember

- A large friction force is needed for good grip.

- Water reduces the friction force between two surfaces.

Electrical Circuits and Conductors

Electrical Circuits

Electricity comes from the mains or from cells.

For something to use the electricity it has to be part of an electrical circuit.

In the home there are many different circuits hidden in the walls and the ceilings.

Simple electrical circuits can be made like this:

A

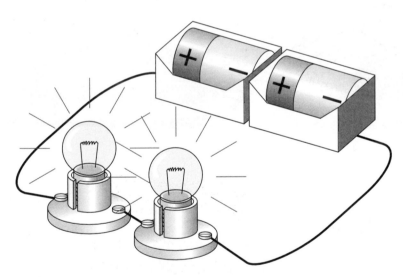

The cells are joined together to make a battery.

There are also two bulbs and some joining wire.

In this circuit there are two cells.

For the circuit to work the electricity must be able to leave one end of the cell, go round the circuit, and return to the other end of the cell.

There must be a complete circuit.

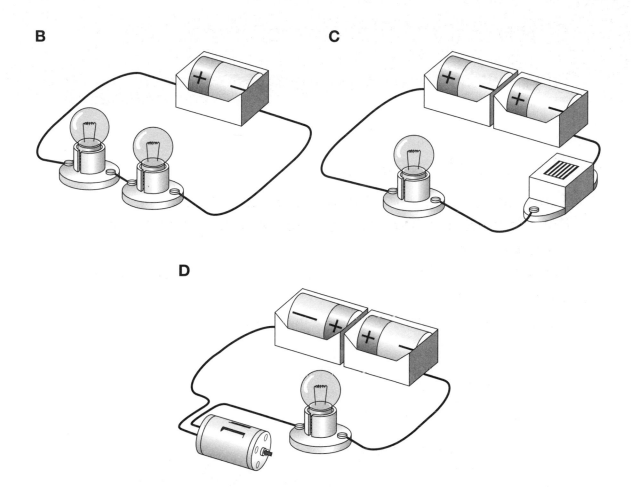

B

C

D

Questions

1 Write down three things that use electricity from cells.

2 Write down three things that use electricity from the mains.

3 Look at the drawings B, C and D.
  a) Which circuit has a buzzer in it?
  b) Which circuit will not work? Why not?

4 Draw a circuit that works with two cells, a motor and a buzzer.

Remember

- Some things use electricity from the mains, e.g. a television.

- Some things use electricity from cells or batteries, e.g. a torch.

- Electricity will only flow if there is a complete circuit.

Electrical Conductors and Insulators

Some materials allow electricity to pass through them.
They are called electrical **conductors**.

Other materials do not let electricity pass through them.
They are called electrical **insulators**.

This circuit can be used to test materials.
If the bulb lights, the material is a conductor.
If the bulb does not light, the material is an insulator.

A

Did You Know?

- In homes, copper is the material used to make the electrical wires. Silver is a better conductor of electricity than copper, but it is too expensive to use.

All metals are electrical conductors.
Other materials like wood, fabric and plastic are electrical insulators.

B

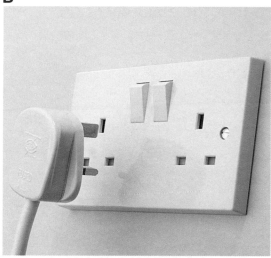

C

The outside case of the plug and the socket are made of plastic. Plastic is an insulator. This means you do not get an electric shock when you touch them.

Copper is used for electrical wires. It is a very good conductor of electricity.

Questions

1 Name three materials that are electrical conductors.

2 Name three materials that are electrical insulators.

3 Look at picture C. Why is the copper wire surrounded by plastic?

4 Why are the three pins of the plug shown in B made of metal?

Remember

- Electrical conductors let electricity pass through them.

- Electrical insulators do not let electricity pass through them.

- All metals are electrical conductors.

More About Circuits

Electrical devices are not used all the time. They can be switched on and off.

Electrical circuits use switches so that the electricity can be controlled.

A

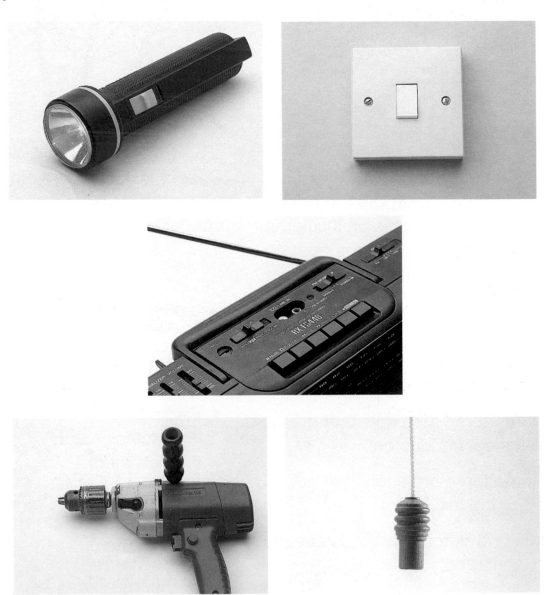

This picture shows different sorts of switches.

Switches can be made quite easily for simple circuits.

B

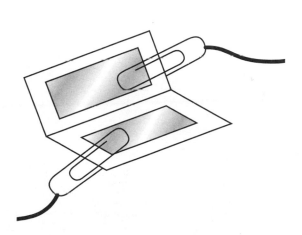

A simple 'press' switch.

C

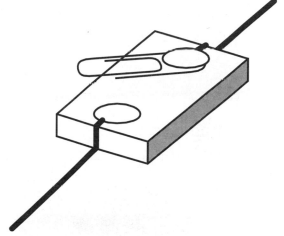

A simple 'flick' switch.

Questions

1 Look at A.
  a) How is the CD player switched on?
  b) Why might a different type of switch be used in a bathroom to the type used in a living room?

2 Look at B.
  a) Why is aluminium foil used in this switch?
  b) Could plastic be used instead?

3 Look at C. Could a matchstick be used in the switch instead of the paper clip? Give a reason for your answer.

Remember

- Switches are used to control the flow of electricity.

- When the switch is on there is a complete circuit for the electricity to flow round.

- When the switch is off there is a break in the circuit.

Unusual Circuits

A

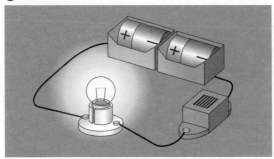

When circuit A is set up both bulbs are quite dim.

B

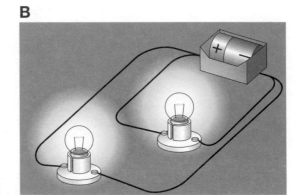

The bulbs can be made brighter by connecting them in a different way. Circuit B is like two separate circuits joined together.

C

The bulb works but not the buzzer! The bulb and buzzer are not matched.

Question

These two bulbs are different.

What is the difference?

Remember

- Bulbs, motors and buzzers need to be matched if they are used in the same circuit.

- A cell can be part of more than one simple circuit.